Deliverance from Darkness into the Light

By
Brenda Pearce

PublishAmerica
Baltimore

© 2009 by Brenda Pearce.
All rights reserved. No part of this book may be reproduced, stored in a retrieval system or transmitted in any form or by any means without the prior written permission of the publishers, except by a reviewer who may quote brief passages in a review to be printed in a newspaper, magazine or journal.

First printing

PublishAmerica has allowed this work to remain exactly as the author intended, verbatim, without editorial input.

ISBN: 978-1-60749-644-1
PUBLISHED BY PUBLISHAMERICA, LLLP
www.publishamerica.com
Baltimore

Printed in the United States of America

*A testimony of my life
and
Praise to my Lord and Savior Jesus Christ*

Table of Contents

Chapter One: The Love of the Lord 13

Chapter Two: The Lord Will Never Leave You or Forsake You 18

Chapter Three: Trials and Tribulations by Choice 30

Chapter Four: God's Amazing Grace 58

Chapter Five: Love and Guidance from My Heavenly Father ... 67

Disclaimer

Throughout this book I have written about specific events that affected my life. These events are written from my point of view, my perspective. However, this book was not written to discredit or demean anyone in any way. These are all events that happened in the past and have long since been forgiven. Even though it is true most have not been forgotten. I don't mean to say that I have not forgotten them out of anger but, I am saying that God has given me the strength and knowledge to know that forgiveness brings peace and joy in my life. The Lord is allowing me to remember specific events in my life to minister to someone else that may be going through a similar situation.

That is the whole reason for writing this book. It is not to hurt anyone, punish anyone or get back at someone. It is merely a tool to help minister the love of God to others who may be hurting or going through similar difficulties in their life. This is why I have put no names in my book other than my grandson's name. I pray that all who read this book, including those who may be included in the book, see this as a hope that no matter what past mistakes we have made, and I'm including myself in this statement, we can ALL be forgiven by God, forget past hurts and have a life filled with peace and love for all. God Bless.

All quotes have been referenced from the King James Version of the Bible.

Introduction

I dedicate this book to the Lord who has delivered me from the hands of Satan and who has given me eternal life through his supreme sacrifice. I also dedicate this book to my Grandmother who prayed for my salvation and to my three month old grandson J.J. LaBakis who is currently embraced by the hands of God and whom I will one day see as I enter the gates of Heaven.

This book is written to share the testimony of how the Lord has touched my life and changed me from what I was to who I am now and forever. This book has been inspired by my love of the Lord God almighty. It is my prayer that whoever reads this book will learn through my trials and tribulations and see that through the acceptance of the Lord Jesus Christ that He can give a glorious life of peace, joy and love.

My prayer is that you will allow your heart to be opened and receptive to the voice of the Lord and allow him into your heart and enjoy and embrace the grace and mercy of God and his love. Amen.

Deliverance from Darkness into the Light

Chapter One
The Love of the Lord

I heard a television evangelist say during one of his sermons that God made us to love him and God also made us for him to share his love with us. Throughout various stages of my life I had tried to understand the concepts of something called "love." The words "I love you" were words I only heard and experienced during the times our family would go and visit my grandparents. The words "I love you" weren't spoken at home.

As a young child trying to understand this thing of love was often confusing for me. I didn't understand why I would feel such compassion for something or someone in my heart and then later be hurt by it. It never made sense to me how the people that were suppose to be the ones to love and protect you were the ones who seemed to hurt you the most. I had always believed as a child that love was something wonderful, not hurtful. However, as time passed and things began to happen in my life and I got older the dream of love and trying to find this thing called love became an important focus in my life. Yet, all I ever found was more disappointment and hurt. I just wanted something to fill my heart and my life with joy and help me feel full instead of so empty. It wasn't until I found the Lord that I found the fullness and true meaning of that wonderful thing called LOVE.

As a young girl life was something that was suppose to be filled with innocents and happiness. However, my life was a life filled with confusion, hurt, shame, anger, mistrust and doubt because I didn't understand all the anger that was in our home. There were many times I would wake up in the middle of the night hearing my parents argue and fight. I remember many times, when my parents were together, that I would just wish they would go away so that I wouldn't have to hear them fight anymore.

As a young girl, about eight years of age, I remember my family and me getting ready to go to my grandparents home in Telluride, Colorado. I loved my grandparents and loved going to their home. Their home was always filled with joy, peace, love and such happiness. It was during this time I decided to bring something with me so that I could bring some of that home with me. I searched all over the house to try and find something to capture the essence of the joy, peace and love that was in my grandparents' home and bring it to our home and then maybe our home would be that way too.

I continued my search and as I was in the bathroom getting my toothbrush I noticed a small brown medicine bottle with an eye dropper in it. It was small yet I thought well it might be big enough to hold it all. So I packed that little brown medicine bottle in my little suitcase and when we arrived at my grandparents house I opened the bottle and sat it on the head board of the bed and told my older sister not to touch it. She just looked at me like I'd lost my mind. Yet, I didn't care. I knew that somehow I had to capture this peace, joy and love and bring it back to our house.

As we got back home the same dread came over me as my parents began to argue and the fights continued yet, a part of me was alright because I knew I could go to my room where I hid that brown medicine bottle and just open it up and feel the peace, joy and love that I brought back with me from my grandparents home. For many years after, I continued this ritual every time we went to my grandparent's home.

Looking back now I know to some people it may seem so strange for me to have tried to capture such an essence in a medicine bottle. However, as God was trying to show me then as that young child He continues to show me today. When there are times of trouble I have a place to go to find peace, joy and love whenever and wherever I need it and I don't have to try and capture it in a bottle. He gives it freely whenever I need it. I just go to Him.

> *We love him, because he first loved us. (1 John 4:19)*
> *Herein is love, not that we loved God, but that he loved Us, and sent his Son to be the propitiation for our sins.*
> *(1John 4:10) KJV*

I never heard the words "I love you" from my parents and I was never told that I made them proud when I tried to do something good. I didn't understand why I would hear other parents say those words to their children, yet my parents never said them to me. I didn't understand what it took to make parents proud of their children.

I would see other kids do things for their parents and get hugs and an "I'm proud of you," from their parents, yet I didn't receive it from my parents. I know this must sound like I'm feeling sorry for myself but it's not meant to come across that way. As a young child these things are important and it is just the beginning of how the Lord can take such a gloomy situation and make something so wonderful out of it. Just wait and see.

The Lord is always with us even in times we don't think that he is. The Lord began working in my life from the time I was born, yet I can only look back and remember from the time I was eight years of age and reflect and ponder how the Lord was speaking to me, guiding me, holding me up and even loving me through all my trials and tribulations. It was during my trials and tribulations that the Lord was with me and with the help and love of the Lord it was those trials and tribulations that eventually molded and formed me into who and what I am today. Even to this day, the Lord continues to guide me, teach me, speak to me and love me through it all.

Chapter Two
The Lord Will Never Leave You or Forsake You

I'll begin with the first time the Lord began speaking to me and trying to let me know he was with me. I was eight years old and my family and I were visiting my grandparents in Telluride, Colorado. My older sister and I were playing with this young girl about our same age. She and her mother were living in the house next door to my grandparent's house. The young girl invited my older sister and me to come over to her house and have lunch. We asked my grandmother and she said it was fine.

I remember entering the house into a small kitchen area with a table that sat four chairs. The table was set with four plates, glasses and on each plate was a sandwich and chips. The glasses were already filled with something to drink. As my sister, the young neighbor girl and I were getting ready to eat our lunch the young girl's mother sat down in the chair across from me and reached out and took my left hand as I was reaching for the glass with my right hand. The young girl's mother looked me in the eyes and told me that I had the power to fight the evil around me and that I had the power to fight Satan.

I didn't understand what she was talking about. I was not raised in church and didn't have the understanding of the Lord in my life. I thought this woman was a nut. I thought she was crazy. I began to ask myself why she would tell me something like that. Yet, in the back of my mind I had a sense that she was telling me the truth, a truth I didn't know or understand yet. I had a feeling or a sense that I needed to trust her words and know that what she was speaking was the truth. It would not be until I accepted the Lord at the age of 36 that I would then begin to know and understand how true those words were.

The day those words of truth were spoken to me a seed was planted that would eventually give me the strength to fight all the evil that Satan tried to throw my way. I didn't know the Lord then like I know the Lord now but, HE already knew me and He knew just what I would need to have victory in my life.

Oh, just a little side note…a few months later when my family and I went back to visit my grandparents, my older sister and I had asked my grandmother if the little girl still lived next door. My grandmother replied she didn't know where they were. She hadn't seen them in a while and she didn't remember them ever moving out of the house. They weren't there any more and someone else had moved into the house. My grandmother stated that it's almost like they hadn't been there at all.

It would be a year later that those words of fighting Satan would come to pass. My innocent's was taken away by my father at nine years of age. My father molested me during the times my mother was at work. It became a ritual every day after school I knew I was to meet my father upstairs in the master bedroom and then I was to go downstairs and pretend that all was well with the world. Over the course of five and a half years of constant abuse from my father I could feel my life just drain from me.

I began to not care about myself. As I got older and became a young teenager I didn't care what I looked like, what clothes I wore. I can remember all the girls at school and some of my friends, those few I had, would all talk about the latest fashions and boys and all those things a young teenage girl is concerned with during that time of her life, I just didn't care. I became so bitter and angry at the world. I didn't trust anyone and didn't care or want to care about anyone or anything.

At the age of fourteen my older sister had met a young boy

who attended a local Church of Christ. He had invited my older sister and me to attend a youth group on Wednesday and Sunday nights. There were even times that we would attend devotions on Saturday nights. I felt such a peace in my life when I would attend the devotions and even when I walked in the church doors. I felt safe and I wanted so much to learn more about this Jesus, the one that every one went to when they would pray about their problems. Yet, the discouragement and despair would soon return as soon as I went back home and I would feel such hopelessness.

I remember sitting up many nights after my father had molested me and my mother would come home and something would happen. Then my parents would be up half the night fighting and arguing. I would open my bedroom window on the nights the moon was full and the moonlight would be shining so bright in my room that I would just sit on the side of my bed and lean against the window and just try to talk to this person they called Jesus.

I would press up against the window and just imagine I was pressing up against someone's chest and pretend that there were someone's arms wrapped around me and telling me that all would be alright, that everything was going to be okay. I would just stare at the moon and pretend that it was the face of this person named Jesus. Little did I know that the Lord was looking down on me, holding me and loving me and that the peace I was feeling was the peace, He the Lord Jesus Christ so desired for me to have in my life. God had already planted the seed of hope and had begun the process of molding my life. I just didn't know it yet.

It was a few weeks later and my days were the same as usual. I had been having a bad day and really began to feel such despair and hopelessness in my life due to continued situations at home. Then one day my older sister introduced me to a young man. He was tall, dark hair, dark eyes and handsome. I had just turned fifteen at the time and was not used to anyone giving me any kind of positive attention. He asked me out on a date and for the next year we were an item.

I began to feel that maybe my dad was wrong and that I was made to be more than just the whore he told me I was made to be. I began to feel something inside of me that felt good and pretty. Something I had never felt before. Until I found out that the only reason my boyfriend was going out with me was to sleep with me. Well, it wasn't until after we had slept together that I had found this out and things changed. I confronted him with this and he said it was true and he did say that he felt bad.

It was also during this time I found out I was pregnant and knew I couldn't tell my parents. I was so afraid my dad would beat me and kill my child or make me get an abortion. I knew there was no way I would ever let him harm my child. I knew then that this child was going to know it was loved and have a life unlike mine. I never told anyone I was pregnant not even the young man. I was afraid to tell. I hid it the best I could. There were many times I would hide in my closet the closer it got to the time to deliver my child I would just cry and tremble, wondering and being so afraid of what might happen to my child. The last three months were the worst.

I tried to make sure I didn't eat much, wore tight pants and loose shirts and I really pulled it off until one morning at five a.m. I began having pains, they felt like gas pains. I was sixteen at this time and I didn't know what was going on. I didn't even think it was time to deliver my baby yet. I stayed in my room for awhile then my mother came in before she went to work and said she wanted us up and make sure our chores were done before she got home today. By this time the pains began to get a little worse. My older sister kept telling my mom that she needed to get me to the hospital, but I just told my mom it was a slight stomach ache and I would be fine.

I then got up and went to the bathroom and sat on the toilet and that's when it happened. I pushed once and there she was, a beautiful baby girl. All I remember was hearing her cry in the toilet. My older sister came in and lifted me off the toilet. She got my daughter out of the toilet and helped me to the floor. I remember my sister handing me my daughter and hearing my youngest sister yelling, "I'm an Aunt! I'm an Aunt!" My mother and dad came downstairs to find me on the floor of the bathroom holding a small baby girl. The next thing I remember was the paramedics talking to me and asking me some questions.

I then woke up in a hospital room with my daughter next to me in an incubator. She was so beautiful. I knew right then and there I had a purpose in my life and something to live for. I had no idea at this time just how God really did bless my life. I knew then that I had been given a great gift, but I didn't know that God was going to use this gift to guide me home to my Lord and Savior.

My daughter was born July 18th, 1979 at home in the toilet in Albuquerque, New Mexico. She weighed six pounds four ounces and was nineteen inches long. It was a day I would never forget. Neither would my family.

A nurse had come into my hospital room asking me about the name of my baby to put on the birth certificate. I still had no name for my daughter. Shortly after the first nurse came in, two wonderful nurses came in and brought me a book of names to look over. I saw a name Christina, in this book it meant strong sword for Christ. For some reason this really struck in my heart and I knew with no doubt this was her first name then her middle name was after my mother and my older sister.

The nurse came in and asked who the father of the child was and I said just leave it blank. I thought he didn't want to be a part of her life then he won't be a part of her life now. Three weeks later my older sister came in my bedroom and told me she had contacted the father and he was on his way over to see my daughter. He came and brought diapers and formula and asked if I needed anything. We went out a few times.

My mother and dad asked that we go talk to a pastor at the Church of Christ. We did and while sitting in the lobby while the pastor talked to him I heard the pastor ask, "Do you want to marry her?" his reply was "No." It was at that moment I felt all the hurt, anger, rejection, filth and knew that maybe my dad really was right. I will never amount to anything more than being a whore. This thought and feeling just flooded my whole being and it was all I could do to walk in the pastor's office. I just became numb and never wanted to ever feel for anyone ever again. I also told the pastor that I didn't want to marry. We left his office and it was shortly after that, I never saw him again.

A few months past and my life seemed so busy with working, school and raising my daughter. My dad left me alone and was gone from the home a lot due to a new job he had taken. Life seemed to be going alright. I was still trying to figure out just how I would manage to leave home. It seemed even more difficult with a child now.

Then one day I was invited to go to a Saturday night devotional with my sister and one of her friends. So I went and I met my soon to be first husband. I wasn't too sure about him at first but over time he said the right things and made me feel like I was special. I then felt like this was my way out of the house and a way to prove to my dad that he was wrong. I was not who he told me I was and I would be more that he told me I would ever be.

We dated for a few months and he asked me to marry him. I was still not sure. Something inside me told me to really think about this, but I just ignored it and knew this was my deliverance from my current situation. So, I hung on with all that I had and was not going to let go. All the wedding plans were set. I had purchased the dress, the cake and the invitations. Then my parents refused to let me get married.

I had no choice because I was not eighteen years of age. I was still only sixteen years old. I had no choice but to cancel my wedding and I couldn't get any of my money back on any of the things I had purchased. It was during this time that my mother and dad decided to have me go talk to a psychologist. They felt

I was having mental difficulties and was not fit to take care of my daughter. I decided then to take action because they were not going to take my daughter from me.

I called a friend of mine at work and asked if she could take me to the bus station. I had spoken with my Aunt in Arizona and asked if I could come and stay with her for a while until I found a place. She said I could. I began packing mine and my daughters things and putting them outside my window in the back yard. My younger sister found the items outside and told my mother. Then the fight was on. My mother wasn't going to give me my daughter. I told her she was not going to keep her from me. The police were called and I got my daughter back. I was told I just needed to leave and if possible leave the state. So I did with my soon to be first husband.

For the first time in my life I felt freedom. I felt like the chains of bondage had been lifted from me. I didn't know then that the decision or choice I was making was actually the decision or choice that was allowing Satan the opportunity to continue in the control over my life. God provided me with several opportunities to make better decisions. I just didn't listen when God was dealing with me in my spirit. Instead I rejected him. Therefore, I rejected his protection.

Some people may think, "How could God allow such a horrible thing to happen to one so young?" Many people want to blame God for the wrongs that go on in their life, just like I did. Yet, if we look back over our situations in our lives and reflect back, how many times did God speak to us and try to guide us? God is continuously trying to guide us through the times of our lives where choices or decisions have to be made and "we" ignore God's guidance.

Some may ask how God could allow a child to be molested. My answer to that question is God was with me the whole time, even though Satan was attacking me through someone else's choice. It was God that gave me the strength to endure and he was building me up to be a great warrior for Him and His purpose. You'll see. What Satan means for bad, God takes it and turns it into something good, if we allow Him.

After I received the Lord and became a Christian, I began looking back over the numerous times God brought me to his house, delivered the word to my heart and spoke to my spirit. However, I was so overwhelmed by the feelings of this world and by the hurt I had been through it was me who rejected Him and his guidance. It was me that allowed Satan to control my life. Therefore, the things that happened to me as I got older were not of God, but the works of Satan through my decisions. However, because of God's unconditional love and persistence I eventually became obedient and turned to my Heavenly Father and came home. I don't intend to ever turn back to the world. I intend to continue being obedient in serving my Lord and Savior and looking up and getting ready to go home to my Heavenly Father where I belong.

Chapter Three
Trials and Tribulations by Choice

For the first year after I left home I stayed with my fiancée's mother. My fiancée was in the military and he had to wait until we were married before he could get base housing. Therefore, I stayed with his mother and took care of her and my daughter until my fiancée and I could get married and move in on base housing. I wasn't eighteen yet we had to get my parent's permission to marry. My Aunt and Uncle in Arizona talked to my parents and after a year they finally agreed and at seventeen I was married.

My husband and I moved into on-base housing and the first month was alright. I noticed he liked to stay out a lot and would come home drunk. One night I asked him if he could just stay home and watch a movie together and he immediately snapped and stated that it wasn't my place to tell him what to do and he wasn't in the mood to stay home when he could have a better time somewhere else.

After a couple of months I found out I was pregnant. He was excited and like most ignorant young girls I thought well maybe this would change him and he would stay home more. Well, things only got worse. He began coming home drunk and angry and began accusing me of cheating on him. Now during this time I wasn't allowed to have the car. I had to walk everywhere while pregnant and carrying my two year old daughter. I wasn't allowed to have friends. If I needed to go to the store I had a time limit to get there and be back.

My husband went out every night. He spent most of the paycheck and during the time I was pregnant I usually ate peanut butter sandwiches and soup so that my daughter had a good meal to eat and he had a good meal. If a hot meal wasn't ready when he got home and sitting on the table for him, he became angry and abusive. He would come in and jerk me out of bed and kick me all the way down the hallway and slap me until the meal was ready and yelling the whole time.

There was a day that his supervisor's wife came to the house to visit me and we had a nice visit but my husband came home for lunch and saw that I had someone in the house without his permission. I knew then that as soon as he got home that night

I was in for it. He got home late that night after being at the bar. I had locked the doors hoping he would not be able to get in. He broke the glass in the doors and broke the front door down. He then came in and grabbed me by my hair dragged me across the living room and began yelling in my face and slapping me.

I was eight months pregnant at this time. I tried to get away from him to protect the baby and get to my daughter. He picked me up and threw me into the coffee table and then drug me on the floor into the bathroom where he picked me up and threw me in the bathtub. He told me to just stay there. I couldn't get up and he came in with his shotgun and loaded it in front of me. He then held the gun to my head and told me he was going to blow my brains out and then kill my daughter. He just kept yelling at me. Then I heard something at the front door.

He got me out of the tub and told me to go answer the door. Now the glass was broken out of the front door, the door was off the hinges; I was eight months pregnant and had bruises and blood on my face and running down my head. The military police were standing at the door and asked if everything was alright. I told them I needed their help. They both looked at me and just told me that I married him and I just needed to handle the situation myself and just keep it down. Then they left.

My husband during this time went to the bedroom locked the door and passed out. I knew I couldn't go to my Aunt and

Uncle for help because my Uncle was an alcoholic and he and my Aunt were in the middle of marital problems as well. I got on the phone and called my mother in Arkansas and asked if there was a way she could help me and get me home. Her words to me were, "You made your bed. You lay in it." Now during this time my mother was going through a divorce and a rough time in her life so I don't fault her for what she said to me and I never have. I was just in hopes that someone would help me.

I hung up the phone and just sat on the floor and cried. I felt so hopeless and had no where else to go and knew no one else to ask for help. I then got up and went to my daughters bedroom where she was sleeping and just held her tight and told myself then that I would do all I could to protect her. I didn't know how I would get out or when but I knew some how and someday I would have to get out.

After my oldest son was born my husband left me alone for a few months. Then it was the constant going out, coming home making sure the meal was on the table, hearing him tell me how ugly, fat and pathetic I was as a person and a wife. He even told me that he wished he had married his high school sweetheart instead of me and he even showed me her picture.

I eventually just gave up thinking that I would ever be more than he and my father said I would be and began believing them. I believed he was right after all. It was the same thing my father told me and now him so therefore, it must be right. I just began believing everything he told me and just became a puppet. He would come home from the bar drunk and tell me all about the women he had danced with and some nights he would come home and tell me how he had slept with a woman and then make a point of telling me how great in bed she was.

Once, I even found pictures laying on his night stand he had taken of one of the women he had slept with. It was a picture of her still lying in the bed. It was like a trophy he brought home to show me. I didn't get upset. I just remember feeling so numb and hearing this voice inside my head saying, "see you really aren't going to amount to anything, you're just a worthless piece of trash to be thrown away."

It was at this point in my life I knew I didn't matter but I had to make sure that I made it a point to let my children know that they mattered. I made it my daily work to let my children know how important they were, how much I loved them and how special they were no matter what anyone else ever told them. I began just living my life for my children.

Over time my husband allowed me to do home daycare. He didn't want me working outside the home but he allowed me to work in the home to make "him" more money. I got my daycare license and when I would get paid by the parents, I would hide some of the money. I had lied to him of how much I charged so that he thought what I was giving him was the full amount. I would take that money and buy my children their school supplies, clothes, shoes and other things they needed. Sometimes it would even be food or toys for them.

I wasn't allowed to buy anything for myself. My wardrobe consisted of a pair of blue jeans, a t-shirt that was his, and a pair of flip-flops for shoes. I had a pair of cut-off blue jean shorts that my neighbor gave me. I had two pair of underpants and one bra. I would ask permission to buy an outfit and was told if I needed something he would get it. Yet, he would come home with new socks that would cost $ 50.00, $100.00 for a pair of shoes and he would get mad if I spend $100.00 for clothes for the three kids for school or necessities for them such as toothbrushes, shoes and even underwear and socks.

He would ask where I got the money to buy it and I would tell him my mother or grandparents sent it so that he wouldn't suspect I was hiding money from him. When I lied and told him where the money came from he got mad but didn't come after me and try and hurt me. I learned quickly how to lie to keep the peace in the house and keep my children safe from hearing the abuse.

It was shortly after my youngest son was born my husband had orders to go to Germany. My husband didn't like the idea of leaving me alone for the three weeks not because he cared but because he was afraid I would reveal who he really was and that I would have the opportunity to take off. I really thought about it during this time. However, it was during this time my grandparents had just bought a home in Mesa, Arizona and had begun visiting and seeing me and their great-grandbabies.

I couldn't let my grandparents know that there was anything wrong. I just didn't want to disappoint them and let them down by showing what a failure I was at providing a peaceful home for my children. I had always wanted and dreamed of being like my grandmother, the perfect wife, mother and grandmother and being able to provide such a happy and wonderful home. So I pretended all was well and went to Germany and spent three and a half years in Germany. I actually loved it.

As I look back over my life it amazes me, even now that I'm a Christian, just how God works. It was three weeks before my children and I were able to go to Germany. My husband had to secure a home and a vehicle before the military would allow the family to be brought overseas. So my children and I stayed at his mother's house while she was away visiting her family in Pennsylvania. It was in mid December when we got the call from my husband that we were to be at the Phoenix airport to pick up our tickets and begin our travel to Germany.

Now at this time my daughter was five years old, my oldest

son had just turned three years old and my youngest son was six months old. I was traveling alone and had two large suitcases, a large bag with changes of clothes and toys for the children, a diaper bag for the baby and a large purse with all our travel information. We were flying from Phoenix, Arizona to Kennedy Airport in New York then from there on to Germany. When we arrived at Kennedy Airport in New York, we were to go from terminal A to terminal B and I had to carry our bags because the airport wouldn't transfer inner continental flight luggage to overseas flights. So I had my three small children, all the carry on luggage and the two large suitcases in a huge airport, in a city I had never been in.

I told my daughter to hold on to my belt loop and not to let go, my oldest son was attached to a harness, I was carrying my youngest son plus the carry on luggage and pushing and pulling the two large suitcases through the Kennedy Airport terminals. There were thousands of people walking past me and not one person stopped to help. As I was about to think all hope was lost, I heard this sweet little voice from behind me. There stood this elderly lady. She asked if I needed help and I told her I would greatly appreciate some help. She took my daughter's hand and my carry on luggage. I took both my boys and the two large suitcases to the next terminal. I kept thanking her for her help and told her I just didn't think I was going to make it on time. She told me that there is always someone there to help if I just ask.

I thanked her again. I asked her where she was headed and she said she was headed to Germany. She told me that she was here in the states visiting her son who just got married and was now on her way back to Germany. I told her that we were on our way to Germany. We reached the terminal with an hour to spare. The flight had been delayed. The elderly lady told me about Germany and how beautiful it was and all the things I should see. We talked and she played and talked with the children. Then the announcement came over the intercom that it was now time to board. As I was gathering my things and heading toward the boarding gate, the elderly lady told me to just hang in there things would get better. I turned to pick up the diaper bag and as I turned to thank her again for all that she had done, she was gone. I looked around in all directions and she wasn't there anywhere.

I thought to myself, I know she was here I just spoke to her how could she move so fast. As the Bible tells us we entertain Angels unaware. God is always with us whenever and wherever we need him. He sends those across our path to help us in times of trouble to give us hope and encouragement when we feel there is no hope at all. He also sends those across our path to give us hope and show us things that can be if we just believe in Him.

After arriving in Germany, we spent the first year and a half in a small German town just about three miles from the base. It was there that God showed me the hope of things that could be. My husband had rented a house from an elderly German couple. They both spoke very little English yet, they spoke it well enough and understood it well enough we could communicate.

When my children and I arrived in Germany it was just a week before Christmas. My husband went and bought a tree but we had no decorations or money to buy gifts for the children. The next day after my children and I arrived in Germany and were getting settled in the house, the little German lady knocked on the door. I opened the door and the elderly German lady was standing at the door with a box and asked if we had any Christmas decorations for the children. I told her we hadn't received our things from the States yet. I invited her in and as we sat in the living room the elderly German lady opened the box and my three children were on the floor just wondering what was in the box. It was like Christmas had already arrived for them. As she opened the box she pulled out the most beautiful Christmas decorations I had ever seen.

There were various kinds of glass ornaments and candle holders to put on the tree. My three children, the little German lady and I all had a marvelous time decorating the tree. When it was finished it was the most beautiful tree I had ever seen. The children were so excited. The elderly German lady began asking the children if they were getting excited about Santa coming and she asked them what they wanted for Christmas. As she was walking back to the door to leave she asked me if we had bought the children any gifts. I knew there were no gifts bought and I didn't know how I would get the money to buy them anything for Christmas this year. I just told her we hadn't had a chance to get them gifts yet.

It would be early Christmas Eve morning and I heard a knock on the door. I went downstairs and opened the door and found a box. I brought the box inside the house and opened it up and inside there was an old antique doll, an old iron cast car made in Germany in the 1940's and a small toy for a baby. I remember just sitting on the floor and crying. My children would have something for Christmas after all. I got up and went upstairs to change. I went next door to thank them for the gifts but they weren't home. So I waited for them to return. As I was taking out the trash they came pulling up in the drive way between the houses. I walked over to them as they were getting out of the car to thank them. Then I heard the loud ringing of the local church bells. I asked them why the bells always rang Sunday morning and Sunday afternoon. They told me it was to make sure the town was up in the morning to go to church and in the afternoon to let everyone know that church was letting out.

They asked me if my family and I went to church. I told them we didn't. It was at that moment for some reason I felt so ashamed. As I went through the day I began to get thoughts of being in a church and what I felt when I was there. I began to think about the times I would feel such peace and it seemed as though all my troubles just melted away when I was there. I began to wonder how I could talk my husband into going to church. Despair began to overcome me because I knew he would never allow us going to church. I pushed the thought of going to church deep to the back of my mind. Yet, God kept bringing it back in from time to time.

It would be Easter and again there was the despair of not having anything for my children to celebrate the Easter Holiday such as the traditional coloring Easter eggs, hiding the Easter eggs and even waking up and finding the Easter baskets left by the Easter bunny. Then there came a knock at the door bright and early Easter morning just as the church bells rang. I woke up and went down stairs and there stood the elderly German couple bidding me to get the children and come to the back yard. So I went upstairs quickly got the children bundled up and went downstairs to meet the couple. My husband, three children and I followed the elderly couple to the back yard and there in their vegetable garden were three piles of chocolate lying on imitation grass. There were also various colored eggs lying in the grass in the back yard for the children to put in their Easter baskets they had for them on the other side of the garden.

The elderly couple just stood there with smiles as the children screamed with delight and began finding the eggs and putting them into the baskets along with the piles of chocolate. I just stood there crying and hugged them both and thanked them for all that they had done. The elderly German lady asked my husband and me if we were planning on going to church today. My husband quickly said no, all of a sudden I felt this wave of shame and guilt come over me. I didn't understand what was happening. A part of me knew this was a day we should be in a church.

Life went on and the elderly couple kept surprising us with so many wonderful gifts and took such good care of me and my children when my husband was gone on temporary duty assignments. When I was around them it was like being around my grandparents all over again. There was such peace, joy and love in their home. There were times the elderly lady would come and ask if my daughter could come over and spend time with her. She would teach my daughter how to make German bread and cook different types of German foods. She would often times take her to the market with her and buy her and the boys toys. They were such a blessing and a sample of the kind of family life I wanted my children to know and grow up around. There were times I would have thoughts that I was such a failure because I wasn't providing that type of home life for my children. Then I would get a thought or a feeling that came over me that would tell me just wait it will come if I just hold on and believe. It would be a year and a half later and we moved into base housing. I really didn't want to move but my husband insisted. Every now and then my children and I would go and visit the elderly German couple when my husband was away on temporary duty.

There are times when God sends people into our lives to show us what we can have if we just turn to him. It's up to us whether or not we want to accept what he has to offer or reject it and continue on the downward spiral to nowhere. It was during this time that God had sent the elderly couple to me as a reminder of what I could have and the life I was supposed to have. Yet, I continued to reject what he was trying to tell me. I continued to reject Him. I continued to listen to Satan and believe the lie that I just wasn't good enough to have a life like that.

My husband was gone on temporary duty assignments a lot. Of course, he was having quite a time away with his buddies and with other women. I on the other hand was having quite a time with me and my children going places and doing things together with them. I continued with the home daycare and was able to help at the school and really be a part of my children's lives. For the first time, I wasn't restricted in being a part of life and all the great things that go along with really being a mother. I had freedom to live and laugh with my children. The times my husband was home I went back into the mode of putting on the show and then when he left it went back to being the real thing of real happiness and joy with my children.

It was during this time I would feel like I was worth something because of my children. I would, for the first time, feel a sense of freedom from a bondage I was so use to. Yet, I wanted to break away from but didn't know how. It was during the time we were living in Germany and I was getting involved in my children's lives that I asked my husband if I could go to college to become a teacher. He just laughed at me and stated I was too stupid to ever do anything like that. Yet, I knew deep within I was going to become a teacher and be successful even though I didn't know how or when, but I had a sense it was going to happen.

DELIVERANCE FROM DARKNESS INTO THE LIGHT

There are many times in our lives when we get a sense or a feeling that it is actually God speaking to us. However, there are also times when we get a sense or a feeling that it is Satan trying to detour us from the direction God wants us to go. That is where we have to go to God and allow him to guide us and not depend upon ourselves for the understanding,

> *(Hast thou not known? Hast thou not heard that the everlasting God, the Lord, the Creator of the ends of the earth, fainteth not, neither is weary? There is no searching of his understanding. He giveth power to the faint; and to them that have no might he increaseth strength. Even the youths shall faint and be weary, and the young men shall utterly fall: But they that wait upon the Lord shall renew their strength; they shall mount up with wings like eagles; they shall run, and not be weary; and they shall walk, and not faint. Isaiah 40:28-31). JKV*

For those who have not accepted the Lord into their hearts, like me during this time, it can be difficult to find your way because there is no knowledge of Him. God still has the ability to speak to our heart and to our spirit. Yet, many times Satan wins out because we continue to reject the guidance of God. It is even during these times when we reject God and his guidance that God continues to love us and will bring about events that guide us in a direction of hope if we just allow ourselves to stop and listen.

God will guide us into a place of blessings that bring about peace and joy beyond our understanding. It's just a matter of accepting him into our hearts and believing and trusting in Him. God provides us a choice of death or life and it is our choice to reject him and find death or accept him and have the choice that can and will not only change your life but give you eternal life of hope, peace, joy and love.

It was during the time in Germany that God gave me a small sample of that peace and joy that he wanted for my life. Now it was up to me to seek after it. God was there waiting on me to accept what he was offering. All I had to do was to reach out and take it.

After spending three and a half years in Germany the orders came in for us to return to the states. The orders were to Albuquerque, New Mexico. We got our house on base and began to get settled in and I began my home daycare up and began watching kids. My husband spent no time in meeting the neighbors and finding those who liked to party. Unfortunately, his best party buddy just happened to be next door. It was no time at all and that's where he was all the time. Of course, I didn't mind at least it kept him out of my hair but it also kept him away from the children.

After we had moved in, I began thinking about going to the Church of Christ where we first met. I asked if I could take the kids to church. He said it was fine if I went and the kids he just wasn't going to go. So, one Sunday morning me and the kids got up and went to church. When we got home the kids talked about what a good time they had and I began talking about us going on Sundays as a family. He just blew me off. That afternoon there was a knock on the door. One of the deacons from the church came by for a visit to welcome us to the neighborhood. My husband and I visited with him for a while and when he left my husband made it quite clear that we were not to go back. He didn't want a bunch of religious nuts coming to his house and he didn't want that kind of satanic influence on his family. He felt Satan was real but God was not real. So the kids and I weren't allowed to go back to church.

I went back into the mode of putting on a show for his friends and his mother. His mother came to live with us for a short time and would often times tell me just how I needed to be running the house. My husband would give her money so that she could go out and go to the bars and have gas in her car. He took real good care of his mother, yet couldn't spend anything on his own wife or children.

I continued hiding money from him to provide for me and the kids. I eventually talked my husband into letting me work outside the home. I convinced him that I could make more money than I was making in home daycare. I began working for a security firm. Well, it went well for a few months and then I got hurt. I went to several different doctors and after hiring a lawyer and fighting out of court I had received my workers compensation check in the amount of ten thousand dollars. Needless to say it didn't take my husband long to spend that money.

It was also during this time that his mother went back home to Arizona and my husband begun making trips out to "see his mother" or so he said. Then there was a time he just took off and was gone for two weeks. I called his work after he didn't come home the next day. His commander stated that he had taken two weeks leave. I then called his mother. She said he was there but I didn't need to bother him because he was busy. After the second week of calling, I finally spoke with him and told him I wanted a divorce. He said that was fine with him because he'd been seeing his old high school sweet heart and he'd been planning to be with her for a while anyway.

I contacted my mother in Arkansas and asked if there was a way she could help me. She didn't have anyway of helping so I knew I had to try to find a way to do it on my own. So, I asked my husband if he could keep the kids until I got a place. He said he was going to keep the kids permanently. He and I began to argue and he picked me up and threw me out of the house with only the clothes on my back and no shoes. I had nothing. The next door neighbor's wife came over and said I could come and stay with her. She gave me a bed to sleep in and I stayed there until I found a job. After a month, I found a job as a housekeeper for a large apartment complex. The neighbor and his wife got a divorce during this time as well. She and I moved in and shared an apartment to help with expenses. She also was raising a child on her own as well and neither one of us could afford it on our own so we decided to help each other.

I then worked my way up as a leasing agent in the company. It was during this time my ex-husband and I were continuing in our battle of the children. One day I got the call that my grandfather had passed away. This was a real blow along with everything else going on in my life. I couldn't even afford to go to his funeral. It was also during this time I met my soon to be second husband. We met while I was leasing him an apartment.

He and I talked a lot and he was a great listener. He also had been through some of what I'd been through and seemed to understand my situation. So he and I moved in together and I began working as a waitress. After six months I was married for the second time. I couldn't believe that I had married again.

I was still fighting for my children and seemed to be making head way.

One day I went to go get my children from my ex-husband from the base, only he didn't show up. After I finally contacted his commander, I found out he was let go from the military and had taken off with my children. I then contacted the district attorney's office to find out what I could do. He stated that until I could prove that he had taken off with my children out of state he couldn't do anything.

During this time, my second husband had hurt his back. A large water heater had fallen on his back and he had back surgery. He also began drinking heavily. I then found out from his sister that he had a drinking problem. He also had a young son who I was taking care of. It then became a situation where I had to protect his son from his own father. I would tell his parents of what was going on and instead of trying to help they just told me to stop aggravating the situation and just deal with it.

So now I was dealing with another abusive situation, the loss of my children and trying to get them back. It was during this time that my grandmother became ill during her visit to New Mexico. One afternoon I got a call from my grandmother and she asked if I'd like to have lunch with her. So my grandmother and I went to lunch. I had such a wonderful time and it felt so good to be with my grandmother. I knew something was wrong yet; I just pushed it aside and didn't want to deal with it.

After I had dropped my grandmother off at my Aunt and Uncle's house and returned home I received a call from my Uncle stating that my grandmother was on her way to the hospital they thought she might have had a heart attack. I didn't even ask to go I just got my purse and out the door I went. I stayed the night at the hospital. The next morning my mother came in from Arkansas. My mother, my Aunt (my mother's sister), Uncle and I were all in the waiting room. The nurse and doctor came out to tell us that she did have a heart attack and it didn't look good. I just didn't want to accept the fact that my grandmother might pass away. I became numb and didn't even hear anything else that was said.

I remember asking the doctor if I could go see her. The doctor said that I could go see my grandmother. As I was walking down the hall I remember hearing a voice reading some words about safety, love and comfort. I knew then that it was someone reading to my grandmother. As I walked in the room my grandmother was sitting up in bed and the nurse was reading from a book that my grandmother cherished. It was the Bible. As I walked closer to my grandmother's bed she smiled at me and introduced me to the nurse. Then she asked the nurse if I could have the Bible and my grandmother asked if I would read her the twenty third Palms. So I opened the Bible and my grandmother helped me find the twenty third Palms. I then sat in the chair next to her bed and began to read from this Bible. While I was reading, it was as though I was in a different world. The words seemed to overcome my most inner being and surround me in such a way that all I could hear around me was my voice saying those words of comfort and peace. It was as if the whole world around me just seemed to fade away. As I finished reading I laid the Bible down on the table next to my grandmother and just sat and watched her while she slept. She looked so peaceful. Through the next week my whole focus in life was my grandmother. It was as if I was trying to hold on to the one thing I knew I had left that brought joy in my life. I just couldn't lose that too.

After four days the doctor came to us and told us that her kidneys were shutting down and now it was just a matter of time. They moved my grandmother to a private room to wait out her time until she would pass on. I just wouldn't accept the fact that I was soon going to lose her too. My Uncle tried telling me that I needed to go home. My Aunt, Uncle and mother were all telling me that it was time to just let her go and let her move on. She was just waiting for me to tell her good-bye. I just couldn't seem to let go. Then while sitting next to her bed something came over me and let me know that where she would go from here would be so much better than where she was now.

I just sat there and watched her sleep and knew in my heart it was time to let go. I bent over, kissed my grandmother on her cheek and told her good-bye. I then told my Aunt and Uncle and mother that I was going home for a while but that I would be back. As soon as I got home, I received the call that my grandmother had passed. I asked my Uncle when and he said shortly after I left. He said it was as if she was just waiting for me to let her go and tell her good-bye. All I remember is hanging up the phone, falling to my knees and screaming out in such despair to this God that my grandmother loved so, why, why did he have to take her from me? Why did he need her when I needed her most? I became so angry and bitter at this God. I didn't understand how such a powerful being could need her when I needed her more. I began yelling, crying and screaming out that I hated God. I kept repeating this over and over and crying out. I remember walking down the hallway to the bedroom and slapping at the walls with such anger and hurt. I felt such despair, loneliness, darkness and numbness. I remember going to the bedroom and locking the door curling up on the bed and crying.

Here I was in another abusive situation, lost my children, broke, no one to help me, lost the only person in my life that gave me hope of happiness and now even that was gone. Why was I here? What else did I have to live for? Then my husband came home from the bar, my step-son came home from school. I went and made dinner and cleaned up. My mother in law came and got my step son for a while and during that time my husband began getting upset and telling me I just needed to get over it.

He became drunk and angry and for the first time I yelled back. I just didn't care any more. I didn't care what he would do to me. He grabbed the shovel handle that he kept behind the bedroom door and began hitting me on the back with it. Then pushing me down the hallway and slapping me, yelling at me, pulling my hair and yanking me to the floor and kicking me. This went on for a while until he got tired and passed out on the couch. I then went to the cabinet where he kept his prescription medicine and took out the bottle of his pain medication. I remember opening the bottle and pouring the bottle of pills in my hand, getting a glass of water and walking to the bedroom and closing the door. I kept hearing a voice tell me don't do it, don't do it. Yet, I just wanted all the hurt to stop once and for all. I just didn't care. Everything that I loved and cared about was now gone. I had nothing else.

I took the handful of pills. The next thing I remember was being in a place that was so dark and I was so afraid. I wanted out. I remember someone holding me down and not letting me out of the place I was at. It was as though I could hear myself screaming and saying profane words I'd never said before yet, my mouth wasn't moving. I kept screaming, wanting out but this thing wouldn't let me go. It just kept holding me down. Then the next thing I remember was waking up in a hospital room where a nurse was standing over me and told me I had been out for a couple of days. I was hooked up to all kinds of tubes and monitors. Then a woman came to my room. She was a psychologist. She began asking me all kinds of questions about my home life.

All I remember saying was, "I want to go home." Now, as I was saying this, I kept asking myself, why I wanted to go home so bad. Home was the last place I wanted to be. Yet, deep inside me it was a home I hadn't been to yet. Something inside me was telling me I would soon be in a home where I have always wanted to be. I just needed to be strong and to listen. My husband was allowed to come into the room and he told her about the loss of my grandmother. He also told her about the situation with my children, but he failed to mention the abuse he was putting me through.

I don't know to this day for sure what happened when I arrived at the hospital. I just know that there was something there that didn't want me to come out of the hospital. Yet, there was something else there that helped me to overcome the situation. I can't explain it and may never be able to explain it. All I know is, it happened and after that I became a person I never knew I could be. I became "Strong."

After a couple of days I returned home from the hospital. I was home and my husband came home from the bar, drunk and was demanding dinner right then and there. I just sat on the couch numb and saying nothing. He then went to grab me and I remember yelling in his face and told him if he ever touched me again I would kill him. I then got off the couch and got my purse and keys and left the apartment. He came after me and tackled me down out in front of the apartment complex where we lived. The police were called and he was arrested. He kept saying he couldn't believe that I was letting him be arrested. I just stood there with such anger and hatred in my heart and so numb. I turned and went back into the apartment.

While sitting there I called my mother and asked her if I could stay with her for a while until I got my own place. I told her I was leaving and would be there in a few days. During this time, I had been on the phone everyday all day long with the district attorneys office in New Mexico and in Arizona. I never let them have a moment of peace until I heard that they were going to get my children back for me. I explained to them that

I was their mother and I wanted them back and if they wanted to never hear from me again then they were going to have to get busy finding my children and get them back to me. It was a couple of days before I left that I got my older son back. After I had arrived in Arkansas I got my daughter back. It would be a little over a year later before I would have all three of my children back.

Now that I have accepted the Lord as my Savior, I know that it was the Lord that was with me through it all. It was the Lord who delivered me from the hands of Satan who was trying to hold me down and keep me from returning to life, a life God was preparing me for. It would be a life I could never have imagined I would ever have. A life I had often dreamed of but never thought beyond my wildest dreams I would ever have and have so abundantly. God is an amazing God if we totally believe and give our lives to Him.

Chapter Four
God's Amazing Grace

I arrived in Arkansas in December of 1992. I began trying to figure out what to do with this new found freedom I had and how I was going to care for my three children. My oldest son was dealing with post distress disorder due to the abuse his father had put him through. My daughter was dealing with her own emotional distress and depression due to situations her father had put her through. I was still in the process of trying to get my youngest son back during this time.

It was during this time my oldest son was having terrible temper tantrums and going back and forth to various councilors. Eventually, I had to send him to a mental hospital for him to get the help he needed to help him deal with the abuse he'd been through. It was during this time that my sister and brother in law were trying to set me up with a neighbor guy. I was working at a factory at the time and working seventy to ninety hours a week at times just to try and make enough to care for my family.

I explained to them that I wasn't interested in meeting anyone. I was planning on going to school, starting a life for me and my children and the last thing I wanted was another situation with a man. So for many months, I just ignored their suggestions to meet this man. Then one day after I got home from work, showered and was lying on the couch in walked a man and my sister and brother in law introduced me to him. I was still not going to go out with him. We talked and visited, he seemed very nice but I wasn't interested in having another relationship.

Several weeks went by and several times he'd asked me out yet I'd turn him down. Finally, I said we could go out and have coffee and talk. So we went to a small diner and had coffee. We talked about our children, plans for our futures and I made it quite clear that I didn't like drinking and I had been hurt and was not going to be hurt again. We went out a few more times and then he began asking if he could take my son fishing and my oldest son really enjoyed being with him and they seemed to have a great time together.

It was at this point I began thinking that maybe I should give this guy a try. So we went out a few more times and after a period of almost a year we got married. For the first two years it was great. We laughed and had a great time and things were going good. I had begun going to school to become a teacher and he was very supportive of me. He often spent time with the boys and took them fishing and hunting. Then I noticed every once in a while he would come home smelling like beer. I asked him about it and he said that he and some of the guys at work stayed after and had a few beers.

There were several times that we would be at my mother's home for cook outs and family gatherings and he seemed to really enjoy the drinking just a little too much. I had asked him to please slow down on the drinking and he just blew me off. I then became angry and my family began telling me I didn't need to be so hard on him. Over the course of the next five years it just kept getting worse. There was money missing from the account to pay bills that he would spend on buying beer and his whisky. He would come home drunk and pass out.

He began to not want to spend time with me or the kids or his own children. It was all about getting drunk. It became an every weekend occurrence that he was drinking from the time he got up to the time he went to bed. Then one day he came home and told me he decided he was going to start his own welding business. So my mother's boyfriend lent him the money to buy a welding machine. My mother and I made up business cards and I passed them out around town and he began to get calls for jobs. Now, during this time he quit his full-time job to begin building his welding business. When a call would come in he would tell them he would be there on a certain day and never show up because he'd been at home doing nothing but getting drunk.

I was still trying to finish up my last year of school to become a teacher and was working at a motel cleaning rooms. I was also dealing with my daughter and trying to find out why she was so sick. After several doctors and several tests later and a biopsy we found out my daughter had cancer. The cancer was in her chest and all on the right side of her neck and abdomen. It was also during this time that the Lord was dealing with me as well.

There were not many days, if any, that I would have the opportunity to sleep in. Between working, studying, getting my sons to basketball practice, football practice, back and forth to school and just the daily dealings of life that I would have an opportunity to sleep in. However, I often found myself on Sundays, the only day I would have to sleep in, up early and watching the television evangelist. I didn't understand why I had such a yearning and need to listen to them.

One day I was cleaning out my drawers in my dresser and

found a small white Bible. It was a Bible my grandmother had given me when I was four years old at my Aunt's (my mother's sister) wedding. The front cover was worn and part of the cover had begun to come off yet none of the pages were torn or even wrinkled. I opened this small white Bible and began to cry and felt a feeling I hadn't felt in a long time. I was remembering the time I was at my grandmother's bed side and reading the twenty third Palms to my grandmother and the peace I felt as I was reading it.

It was in December of 1999 that I graduated from college with my teaching degree and had begun working at an elementary school. It was a week before the 2000 school year would begin, that I arrived at the school to begin working in my classroom. Each year before school officially starts for the students the teachers are at the school preparing their classrooms and attending meetings. It is also during this time that the local Presbyterian Church always put on a breakfast for the teachers. As I walked up to the doors of the Presbyterian Church I heard this voice inside my head say to me "You don't deserve to enter those doors." I just froze and I had a friend standing behind me who just pushed me forward through the doors and I just entered in and began to cry. I turned around and walked back to the school and just worked in my room.

It would be the next week that we would find out that my daughter had cancer. I remember just waiting until everyone went to bed and I sat out on the front porch and stared up at the stars. I just boldly told God he was not going to take my daughter from me. Like I really had any control of it. I then remember just becoming so helpless and crying and then asking this God to please help me. I didn't know what he was trying to do in my life. I asked him to help me understand it all. I asked him to help me know what to do so that I wouldn't have to lose my daughter. I just sat on that porch and prayed until I remember looking up at the sky and the sun was coming up.

I went to work the next day and just seemed to be so numb and it seemed like every day after. It was just so busy. I had finally graduated from college and became the teacher I had always known I would be. I was busy trying to keep my boys in their sports and still dealing with my husband and his drinking problem and now my daughter. Then a month later we found out my mother in law was also diagnosed with cancer.

I was now taking care of my house hold, a drunk and two cancer patients and working a full time job on top of the Lord dealing with me about getting my life right with him. God doesn't give up and will apply pressure when pressure is needed. Boy did I find this out.

My daughter had just finished her senior year of high school and begun her freshman year of college when she was diagnosed with cancer. During this time she had begun dating a young man. This young man was there with her when she was diagnosed with cancer. It was during the time my daughter found out she had cancer and was concerned about loosing her hair, that her boyfriend and two brothers decided to shave their heads completely bald. When my daughter and I arrived home from the doctors the day my daughter had received her first chemotherapy treatment, we saw all three of them standing on the front porch just as bald as three billiard balls. My daughter's boyfriend was there with her when she got sick from the chemotherapy treatments and would hold her hair out of her face when she would get sick. There were times when he would go to the store for her at three o'clock in the morning to get her medications she needed.

During the time my daughter was receiving her chemotherapy treatments there was a medication she would have to have through a 24 hour pump. During the time she was receiving this treatment through the pump, she would have to be monitored every hour to make sure her temperature didn't rise, she wasn't having any chest pains and didn't become to sick. If my daughter showed any of these signs I had to get her to the hospital immediately due to the possible chance the treatment she was taking might be burning her heart up.

DELIVERANCE FROM DARKNESS INTO THE LIGHT

During this time my husband was too involved with his drinking to be any help at all. So, my daughter's boyfriend would come and stay at the house. My daughter's boyfriend, my two sons and I would all take turns taking my daughter's temperature and monitoring her pump and watching her throughout the night. I knew then as I know now that the Lord had sent this young man to us in a time of need. My husband at the time wasn't even helping me with his own mother.

Eventually my daughter finished her chemotherapy and began radiation when her and this young man became engaged and moved from home. It was also during this time my mother in law passed away and my father in law moved to Las Vegas with his other daughter. I then confronted my husband and stated that I was done. It was time for him to make a choice. It was either going to be the bottle or me. He chose the bottle so I packed up my things and left. My oldest son had graduated and moved to Arizona to find better work. So, it was just my youngest son and me. We moved in with my daughter and son in law for a time until I could find a place.

During this time the Lord was really dealing with me. My youngest son was dating a young lady that was going to church and he had gone with her several times and really liked it. He then accepted the Lord. One day I went to his basketball tournament and the young girl and her mother were there and so was the preacher and his wife. As we talked, they invited me to sit with them and they invited me to go to church. So that Sunday my son and I went to church and the Lord really was applying the pressure. I went the following Sunday and accepted the Lord and found that "HOME" the Lord had told my spirit about many years before. I had finally come home to my Heavenly Father.

It was at that moment that I knew I was where I belonged. I had finally found exactly what I had been searching for all my life. I finally found the feeling of completeness and fullness of peace, joy and love. It was at the moment I accepted the Lord I felt such a weight lift from me and for the first time ever I felt so clean and at peace. Even though I was going through financial troubles and a divorce, it all seemed so minor now and I stepped out of a life of darkness into a life of light and hope.

Chapter Five
Love and Guidance from My Heavenly Father

At this point in my life I new I had finally found the life I never thought I would ever have. I finally had a life of peace, joy and love. It was through my relationship with my Heavenly Father, through my acceptance of Jesus Christ my Lord and Savior. After I had accepted the Lord into my life I wanted to know all there was about God and his son Jesus Christ. I wanted to know what I was supposed to do for God and how I needed to serve him. I would read my Bible daily. I attended Church every time the church doors were open. I even volunteered during clean-up days and teaching children's Sunday school classes.

I was growing in my knowledge and love of the Lord and in His word. Yet, I still felt like I wasn't getting enough, I wanted to know more. One day after church the pastor and his wife invited me to attend a Bible study on a Saturday night. The pastor informed me that they were trying to study the book of Revelation. I told them I would be interested and began attending the Bible study. However, the study didn't last long. Eventually the pastor and others became frustrated with the book of Revelation and decided to study another part of the Bible. Nevertheless, the Bible studies eventually faded out and I was left to study again on my own.

As I continued attending church and teaching Sunday school, problems were still a part of my life. I would often become frustrated and despair would begin to over take me. I would then get on my knees and ask the Lord to help me. There were times it seemed like He wasn't there at all. I began to think I wasn't praying right, or I wasn't doing enough for the Lord so I would work harder and try to study harder. God then showed me through His word that it wasn't my works He wanted it was just "me." God wanted a real relationship with me. So, I began speaking to God as a Father and asking for guidance and thanking Him for delivering me out of the messes I got myself into. I then began to feel such a greater joy in my life. I had finally gained a real relationship with a Father I had always wanted every since I was a little girl. A Father who I knew loved me unconditionally. I finally had a

Father who would always be there for me and never leave me or hurt me.

I remember reading the story about the prodigal son coming home to his father. I was the prodigal daughter who had finally come home to my Father. It was so hard for me the first three years I had been a Christian, to finally accept the fact that I was something special. God really had a time trying to get that through my head. It was difficult for me to remove the last 36 years of hurt from my life. Yet, God was already trying to remove it for me. I just wasn't letting Him. I was holding on so tight to all that hurt, anger, and bitterness and unforgiving that I was still not receiving all the blessings God wanted me to have. God finally smacked me upside the head. What I like to call a "God Smack." God let me know that if I was ever going to have total peace in my life like I wanted, then I was going to have to let my past go and let Him fill my spirit and quit allowing Satan access into my life.

I continued praying and asking for God's guidance in my life. A couple of months passed and I asked my nieces if they would like to attend church with me. They both agreed and began attending church with me. Over a period of several weeks I would go to my sister's house and pick up my nieces and visit for a while. There would be times when I would pick up my nieces that my father would be at my sister's house and the first time I saw him I became so ill it was all I could do to enter my sister's house. God began to show me that I had to forgive if I wanted peace. It took a lot of prayer and tears, but I finally forgave my father for what he'd done to me as a child. After I had been up all night with the Lord praying, crying and just seeking His help, I went to my father's house to speak with him. I entered in and we drank coffee and talked for a while. I then told my father I forgave him for what he did. My father never said he was sorry. There was a part of me that was disappointed in not hearing the words "I'm sorry," from my father yet, it really didn't matter. I was looking for the peace in my heart and the forgiveness from my heavenly father. I had learned through the word of God that if I couldn't forgive my father on earth then my Heavenly Father couldn't forgive me of the wrongs I had done here on earth. Therefore, I just trusted my Lord and forgave my earthly father.

After I left my father's house I felt such a weight lift off my shoulders. As I was driving down the driveway and turned onto the road I had to pull off to the shoulder because I was crying so hard. I had finally been delivered from that awful burden. God was with me and brought me through. I know He was with me as I entered my father's house. He was with me as I sat there and spoke to him and told him I forgave him. God was there the whole time holding my hand and letting me know all was going to be alright. I thanked Him and give Him all the praise and glory for my deliverance from such a burden.

As I came to my sister's house, one day my brother-in-law asked me how come I was so happy all the time, even when times were bad. I just said it was because I had the Lord Jesus Christ in my life. A couple of Sunday's past and my sister and bother-in-law began to attend church with me and finally accepted the Lord as well. It was a glorious day.

Shortly after my sister and bother-in-law had accepted the Lord I had begun dating a Christian man that worked with my brother-in-law. It was during this time that my sister, brother-in-law, the pastor and his wife and I began having Bible studies on Saturday nights. We began studying in the book of Romans. Again over time that faded out due to everyone's schedules and life. So, again I was back to studying on my own. During this time God began to teach me things not just through his word, but through life teachings as well.

There were times I would go to the cabinets and wonder what I would feed my son for dinner. There was not much if anything in the refrigerator and not much if any thing at all in the cabinets. Yet, something would tell me to look again and there would be something there for me to fix for dinner every time. There would be times I needed gas to get back and forth to work and I didn't get paid for another week and I would happen to find a five dollar or ten dollar bill in the bottom of my purse. Coincidence. I know it was God helping me and blessing me. I began to notice during these times of determination to study the "Word of God" and became obedient to His will that things continued to change in my life. I began noticing that I was able to pay my bills and still have some money left over. That had never happened before. I would go to the refrigerator and it would be full of food and so would the cabinets. I was able for the first time to go and buy a few new outfits and a new pair of shoes for the first time in my life. Any clothes that I ever had before had always been second-hand clothes even my shoes.

As Christ Himself taught through various parables, that even his father cares for the birds of the air and the flowers of the field are we not more than these? God loves us and wants us to have so many wonderful things in our lives. It's up to us to believe by faith that He's with us and wants to bless us. God so desires his children to live a life of happiness not just a life that is full of material blessings, but blessings of peace, joy, hope and love. For the greatest of these is love. All we, as His children have to do is just believe by faith and become obedient to His word. It's so easy if we get our self out of the way and begin to put Him first in our lives. Then all we have to do is just let the blessings flow through our lives.

As time went on things got better in my life. My financial situation got better, I was dating a real nice guy, I was working as a teacher and I had such a peace in my life. Life was good. Then a wave came into my life. I began to have health issues. First I found a lump in my left breast and I began having chest pains. Even though I was faced with the possibility of breast cancer, I knew God was with me. The breast tumor was benign. The chest pains were due to stomach issues. God continued to watch over me. I was then confronted with a situation at the church I was going through. I knew I couldn't talk to anyone in the church about it because I didn't want to cause a problem in the church. I began to see things I didn't agree with and had issues with. So, I prayed for several months for God to guide me and He told me it was time to move on. When I explained to the pastor that God was guiding me to somewhere else, he stated that sometimes when we think it's of God it's actually Satan. I didn't even respond. I just walked out.

I then began to pray for God to guide me to where I needed to go to continue in his work and serve His purpose in my life and for others. I began going to the church that my boyfriend at the time was attending. I had attended that church for about a year. Then he and I parted as friends and I began to ask God again where He wanted me to go. I then called the local

Freewill Baptist Church just down the street to find out what time their Sunday school started. I got the answering machine. The next day a lady from the church contacted me and informed me of the church times. That next Sunday morning I went to my grandson's dedication at another church, but I went to the local Freewill Baptist Church that evening. As I walked in the doors and sat in the back pew, I knew that's where I was supposed to be.

It was during the service that a man from in front of the church had turned around and looked back my way, when I heard a voice tell me that's the one you'll be with. I then told myself that I wasn't there to gain a relationship with a man I was there to gain in my relationship with God. As the service drew to a close and the invitation was given the same man went to the altar. I then heard the voice again say to me, that's the one you'll be with. I just blew it off and never thought about it again. However, as time went on God insured me that I wasn't going to just "blow it off."

It would be after I began attending the church that I came home after working at school and attending to fifteen students at a Valentine's Day party, when I received a call from my youngest son who informed me that my three month old grandson Jonathan was dead. I remember just being in shock and screaming back at my youngest son telling him that it wasn't true and asking him again what he said. I kept on telling him it couldn't be. Once he got me calmed down he proceeded to tell me how Jonathan passed on. My oldest son had just gotten off of work, after pulling double shift from working at a prison, and my daughter-in-law was leaving for work, that my oldest son fell asleep with Jonathan on his chest. When my oldest son woke up he realized that he was lying on Jonathan and jumped up and Jonathan was not breathing. My oldest son tried giving him mouth-to-mouth resuscitation and then called 911. Once the ambulance arrived my oldest son informed me, during the funeral, that he just sat next to Jonathan's walker and held on to it praying to God save my son, just save my son.

Nevertheless, Jonathan passed on into the arms of God. My oldest son became very bitter and angry toward God because of the passing of Jonathan. He also blamed himself for killing his son. My mother and sisters all told me that when I went to the funeral that I didn't need to preach to my son I just needed to be there for him. I was told specifically NOT to mention God at all. Well my response was that I wasn't qualified to be a preacher and if the Lord gave me the words that my son needed to hear then the words were going to be spoken by God through me and there was nothing they or myself could do about it and I left it at that.

During my time in Arizona while attending Jonathan's

funeral I was informed by my ex-husband, that I was not to mention God or "preach" to my oldest son. I knew I would be facing some opposition while I was there due to the fact that everyone's life style consists of dealing with any problem through alcohol. My response to them was I wasn't qualified to be a preacher and I left it at that. I did read my Bible in front of them. I would also pray before I ate a meal and just sat and listened while they talked and drank.

It was a dark and dreary day on the day of Jonathan's funeral. The mood that morning was of course very somber and not too many words were spoken that morning other than good morning. We all ate breakfast and then loaded up in the vehicles and headed toward the funeral home for the service. No one spoke on the way there and my oldest son just seemed to be in a total fog. As we arrived the tears swelled in his eyes and my heart began to hurt for him so much. I really had to do some heavy duty quiet prayer time on the way there to maintain myself.

As we entered the funeral home a feeling of peace rushed through my body. It was such a joyful peace that I had never experienced before. I walked into the funeral home with my son and daughter-in-law and sat with them. It was very difficult to sit across from a small casket and see this tiny little body lying there and know that I couldn't hold him or cuddle him at that moment. It was so difficult for me to maintain but, God gave me the strength because I know it wasn't my own strength that got me through. After the service we all loaded back into the vehicles and headed toward the grave site and again I did a silent prayer for strength for myself and for my son. During this time the sky was dark and cloudy and it looked like the bottom was about to fall out from the sky. While my son and I were standing at Jonathan's grave site I asked God to please show my son a sign that would give him peace and let him know that his son was safe. Right after I prayed that prayer the clouds right above us opened up and the sun began to shine right over Jonathan's grave. My son looked up in the sky and said, "There he goes." I broke down and thanked God and cried like a baby.

God is so wonderful, even though he knew then and knows now that my son was angry at him and hated him and still has not accepted him. Even at this point God is such a loving God that he still showed my son a sign to give him peace in knowing the truth of where his son is. As my son and I stood underneath the opening in the sky and looked at the sunlight shining through the clouds we both stood in silence and we both knew this sign was from God. Then just as quickly as the clouds opened to receive Jonathan they began to close as to say he's arrived safely home. I then felt such a warmth come over me and I knew it was God letting me know in my spirit he's arrived and he's home.

> *Thou hast turned from me my morning into dancing:*
> *Thou hast put off my sackcloth, and girded me with*
> *Gladness;*
> *To the end that my glory may sing praise to thee, and*
> *not be silent. O Lord my God, I will give Thanks unto*
> *thee forever.*
> *(Psalms 30: 11-12) KJV*

God is always with us and knows what we need when we need it the most. It doesn't matter what the situation or whether we believe or not believe God is always there ready to except us as we are. I know for my son it will take some time for him to accept what has happened and even to accept that God was not the one who took his son away as Satan wants him to believe.

It was at the second year anniversary of Jonathan's passing when I was getting ready for bed. My heart had been so heavy for my son and I knew that my son was having such a difficult time re-living the nightmare of Jonathan's death. As I knelt down to pray I felt such a pressure on my heart. It was so heavy I could hardly breathe and I began to pray. As I was praying I could hear myself begging God to help my son. It was at that moment I laid my head on the bed in such despair and hopelessness, when God gave me a vision, a dream. I remember looking around and the sky was dark and stormy. There was a slight breeze blowing. It was so real that I could actually feel the breeze blowing my hair across my face. I was kneeling and praying and again I could hear myself just begging God to help my son. It was at that very moment I could feel what I thought was rain drops on my shoulders. I then reached up and felt this wet stuff on my shoulders and it felt wet yet sticky like blood. As I looked up to see where it was coming from I saw a man hanging on a cross and as I saw the man on a cross I heard a calming voice say to me, "Do you not believe in me? Do you not remember what I have done for you? Do you not believe that I will do the same for him?"

The Lord then showed me another dream/vision. I found myself standing in a beautiful field. While I was standing in the field I heard the most joyous, light hearted laughter. It sounded like the voices of angels. As I turned around I saw a man sitting on a large white rock and running around him were two small children. One of the children was a small boy about two years of age and a little girl about the age of three maybe four. As I looked closer to the little boy I could see it was Jonathan. He looked just like my oldest son. The little girl had long red wavy hair. She also had a round, chubby face with rosy cheeks and a smile that just lit up my heart. As I was walking closer toward the man and the children, I saw the man turn and look at me. It was Jesus sitting on the rock. The children were running around him, laughing and chasing each other. My Lord was showing me that all was well. There was nothing to worry about. He had everything under control I just needed to trust in Him.

A side note, it would be a few weeks later when I began dating my husband, that the little girl that was playing with Jonathan was his niece that had passed on. When I began describing the little girl to my husband, boyfriend at the time, I told him that she looked a lot like his niece Katie. He then stated that it had to be his niece that had passed on a few years ago. He said that it was about three almost four years since her passing.

It was at this point that I knew that I had to give it all to God. It was at this point when I had learned about just giving all things to God because it wasn't me who was or could change things it was God who could. The moment I gave my son completely over to God I felt such a peace and joy flow through me. The feeling was so indescribable. There are no words that I can say that can ever express the feeling that I felt once I turned it all over to the Lord.

I know that some people may think that I was having hallucinations or that I was in such distress that I only imagined what I saw. I really don't care what others think or believe I know what I saw and I know what God showed me and taught me was the truth. He showed me and taught me that we as mortals have no power or strength to change the world unless it is through the power of the Lord our God for all things good are done through Christ Jesus and given to those who love the Lord. It is through the power of my Lord and Savior Jesus Christ that I found my strength to endure the situation of the passing of my grandson Jonathan.

It is also the strength of my Lord and Savior Jesus Christ that has sustained me through the trials that my children have had to endure such as the situation with my daughter and her cancer, my oldest son with his son's passing, and my youngest son's various situations in his life. Even though Satan knows how important my children are in my life. God is so much more and I know that as long as I keep my focus on Him then everything else in this world will be alright.

God has always provided me with the strength and blessing through any and every trial I have ever had to face and I know even now that He will continue to do so no matter what. God promises that during our trials He will never leave us nor forsake us. God has given me strength in times of weakness,

He has given me comfort in times of uncertainty, God has given peace in times of confusion, security in times of doubt, and His everlasting love, grace, mercy and forgiveness in times of my failures. How, therefore, can I not be true and praise Him for all that He has done and continues to do in my life.

(Psalms 52:8) KJV
But I am like a green olive tree in the house of God: I trust in the mercy of God forever and ever.

(Psalms 136:2) KJV
O give thanks unto God of gods: for his mercy endureth forever.

Throughout my life God has always been there with me. He has always provided anything and everything I've ever needed even during the times I didn't know him. God provided me the blessings I've not deserved, trials to make me stronger, comfort and strength in times of weakness and so much more. God provided all of this even before I accepted Him. There are some that say that God can only do for those who know Him. I believe, through my life experiences, that God is always with us providing us with opportunities to accept Him and showing us who He really is. It is through our denial of who and what

God really is that we give in to what Satan wants us to see and that is the lies that God is the one allowing all these bad things to happen in our lives.

There are times that God allows us to go through things so that we'll wake up and see the truth of His glorious mercy and grace. We just have to allow ourselves to seek the truth but, many times it's easier to accept the lie than it is the truth because when we take a good, long, hard look we find that the truth is we created our own trial. Therefore, it is by our hand and choices that trials may occur but it is God who can take that trial, no matter the situation, and make it into a glorious blessing.

It was my own life's decisions that caused my life to be in such a mess and a total disaster. However, it was God that took me by the hand and cleaned me up as well as my life. He has shown me a life of peace, joy, love that is beyond anything that I could have ever imagined. As a matter of fact the man that God told me "was the one," I'm now married to and he is the most wonderful man that I have ever known. I know that it was due to my obedience to God and my faith in him that I now have the blessings that I have.

I have a wonderful man in my life, a beautiful home that I never thought I would ever have, I have five great children, eight beautiful grandchildren and a great career in education and so much more. I give all my praises and all glory to my Lord and Savior Jesus Christ for his supreme sacrifice that has allowed me the opportunities to have such a glorious life so full of wonderful blessings. I pray for all of those who don't know the Lord that you just allow Him to speak to you. I pray that you let Him in your heart and then you too will experience such a wonderful life. However, it is only through a true acceptance of the Lord that such a life is possible if you just believe in Him.

How wonderful Peter must have felt when he saw the Lord walking on the water and he took the leap of faith and walked on the water toward his Lord. When his focus was on God things were good, when he took his focus off of God his situation changed from joy to despair. If you keep your focus on God and keep Him first in your life then your life will be filled with the glory of God. Just imagine the walk you can have with the Lord.